Craft Workshop

Fabric

Monica Stoppleman & Carol Crowe

A & C Black · London

Designed and illustrated by **Mei Lim**

Photography by **Steve Shott**

Workshop leaders
Carol Crowe for the painted pattern,
tie-dyeing and block printing workshops;
Francine Isaacs for the felt workshop;
Ali Rhind for the rug workshop;
Marcela Eldi de Persus, Karen Robins,
and **Deb Todd** for the appliqué workshop.

First published in 1998 by
A & C Black (Publishers) Limited
35 Bedford Row, London WC1R 4JH

Created by
Thumbprint Books

Copyright © 1998 Thumbprint Books

A CIP catalogue record for this book is available from the British Library

ISBN: 0 7136 4808 2 (hbk)
ISBN: 0 7136 4809 0 (pbk)

Printed in Hong Kong by Wing King Tong Co Ltd

Cover photograph: This appliqué wall hanging comes from
Bihar in north-east India. The scene shows the goddess Durga
with some of her attendants. Their shapes have been cut out of
red cloth, the edges turned in and sewn on to a hessian backing.
Photograph: Collection John Gillow

Contents

Looking at fabrics

Every day, people all over the world wear fabric of one kind or another every day.

In hot places, people wear thin cotton and linen to keep them cool. In cold climates, people wear wool to keep them warm.

People shape and sew fabric into clothes or wind it in lengths around their bodies and heads, like this.

People also use fabric in their homes as decoration, for comfort, warmth and privacy.

Fabric is made from thin strands called fibres. Natural fibres come from plants, such as cotton, flax bushes, bark or even the hair of some animals. Silk thread comes from the cocoons of silkworms.

Some fabrics are made from man-made fibres. Acrylics are made from chemicals which are taken from wood. Nylon is made from crude oil pumped from under the ground.

Fibres can be made into fabric in several ways. Wool can be pressed and rubbed together to make felt. All fibres can be spun into threads which can be either woven or knitted together.

Natural fibres have no particular colour of their own. People all over the world use skill and ingenuity to bring plain cloth to life. They embroider it with coloured threads, dye it in many colours and print it with patterns.

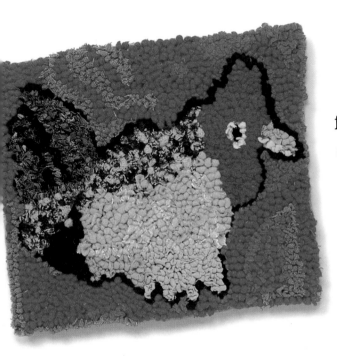

People have even found ways to use fabric several times over by cutting up old clothes and using them to make hangings and rugs. The designs and colours that they use vary enormously. This book shows six ways that you can adapt their techniques to create stunning fabrics of your own.

Look at fabrics around your home, in shops or in books or magazines. Start a scrapbook of pieces that you find attractive. Copy some of the patterns and designs you like into your book. Create your own designs, using bright colours and bold shapes.

Tools and techniques

- Protect your work area with newspaper or a sheet of plastic.

- Wear old clothes or an overall.

- Carefully read the instructions for using dyes, paints and glues before you use them. Check them with an adult.

- Keep a window or door open while you work.

Fabrics

You will need different sorts of fabric for each project. Use cotton or silk for printing, painting and tie-dyeing, since these techniques won't work on man-made fibres. Before you use new fabrics, wash them in hot water, dry them and iron them flat. Collect some coloured and patterned cloth with interesting textures, for sewing appliqués. Try to find some woollen cloth for making rugs.

Dyes

You can colour fabric by soaking it in coloured liquid called dye. You need cold water dyes, silk dyes and fabric dyes for the projects in this book.

It is important to dye fabric in a well-ventilated room and not to breathe in dye dust. Wear gloves and preferably a mask, especially if you suffer from asthma or eczema. If dye gets on to your skin, wash it off in cold water immediately.

Use yoghurt pots or plastic tubs for mixing dye. For soaking fabric in dye, use a plastic washing-up bowl as a dye bath. Make sure there is enough liquid to cover the fabric completely and use tongs or a stick to lift it out.

To increase the absorbency of dye for tie-dyeing projects, soak the fabric in water before putting it in the dye bath.

To dye certain areas only, as in fabric painting, use cold water dyes or silk dyes. These are more expensive, but small amounts will give a strong colour.

Resists

To pattern cloth, you must make a barrier which stops the cloth soaking up dye beyond the intended areas. This barrier is called a resist. Hot wax and gum are the most effective resists. Flour and water paste and clay slip also work.

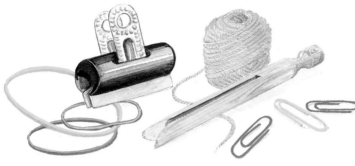

Another way to create a resist is to stitch, tie or peg fabric, so that dye cannot get through the layers at those points. Tie-dyeing works in this way.

Frames

Use an old picture frame for painting patterns on cloth. Tape the cloth on to the frame on all four sides, making sure the cloth is stretched tight and straight.

You can make small proggy rugs on a picture frame, but for bigger ones, you will need to use a special rug frame (see stockists on page 32).

Printing blocks

You can stamp dye on to cloth with a solid object, called a printing block. The colour stays on the surface and does not sink right into the cloth. Use fabric inks or acrylics mixed with textile binder (see stockists, page 32) to make the dye the right consistency for printing.

Here's a simple way to make your own printing block.

Cut two identical squares or rectangles from cork tile or stiff cardboard. Mark matching points on one of the squares, as shown.

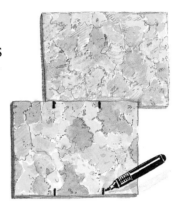

Draw any shape you like between these points.

Cut away the surrounding area and remove the outer pieces.

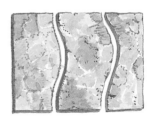

Glue your shape on to the second square or rectangle.

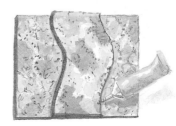

Fabulous felt

Nomads are people who herd their animals from place to place, looking for new pasture. The Kirghiz nomads of Central Asia have made felt rugs like the one below for over two thousand years.

fleece

carding combs

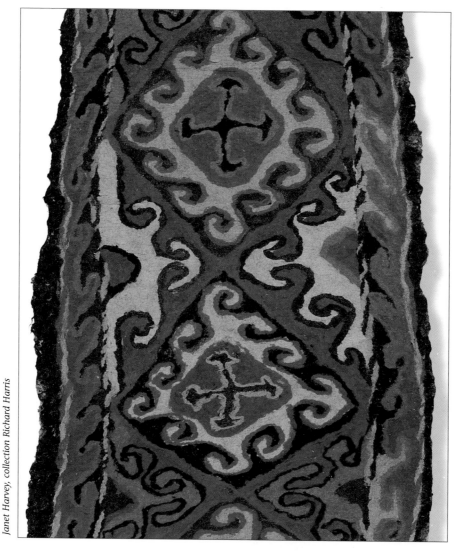

Janet Harvey, collection Richard Harris

sheep's wool magnified 750 times to show the scales on a fibre

Felt is the oldest known fabric. It is made from wool and other animal fibres. These fibres turn into a fabric when they are rubbed together in warm, soapy water. Tiny scales on the fibres lock together and make a flat sheet of felt.

Rulers in their rich palaces and nomads in their tents both value felt for its beauty and warmth. Some claim it has protective qualities. Scorpions and other dangerous insects will never walk across it. However, fleas really love it!

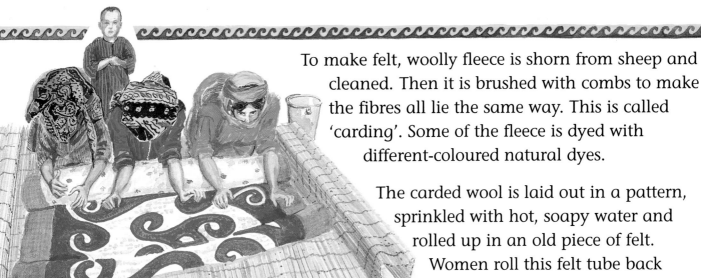

To make felt, woolly fleece is shorn from sheep and cleaned. Then it is brushed with combs to make the fibres all lie the same way. This is called 'carding'. Some of the fleece is dyed with different-coloured natural dyes.

The carded wool is laid out in a pattern, sprinkled with hot, soapy water and rolled up in an old piece of felt. Women roll this felt tube back and forth for hours, pressing down hard with their forearms, until the wool inside the roll has become felt.

Felt clothes are waterproof and very warm. Shepherds in central Asia wear warm felt capes, which they use as sleeping bags at night.

The Kirghiz nomads live in large, domed tents. The outsides are covered with thick sheets of undyed felt, which keep out snow, sun, wind and rain. The insides are furnished with brightly coloured felt rugs, wall-hangings and cushions.

Felting fun

Making felt is simple and exciting to do. It is very wet work, so wear old clothes and work outside if possible. Keep dry work separate from wet work. Buy ready-carded wool for felting from one of the stockists listed on page 32.

fleece

undyed carded wool

dyed carded wool

knitting yarn

Fat felt balls

Wind some thread tightly around a walnut-sized ball of fleece. Wrap ready-carded coloured pieces of wool in different directions around the ball. Then tie some knitting yarn around the ball to hold the wool in place. Put the ball in the foot of a nylon stocking. Tie the end with a slip knot. Dip the ball in hot, soapy water several times. Take the ball out of the stocking and squeeze it again and again. As it becomes firmer, pluck it with your finger and thumb. If no strands of wool lift off, it is has become felt. Rinse and squeeze it several more times. Leave it to dry.

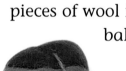

Felt jewellery

Make felt balls of different sizes and let them dry. To make a necklace, thread them together on a length of strong thread with beads in between. Attach fasteners to the ends of the thread.

A felt figure

Stitch together two balls of felt for the head and body. Make felt limbs and sew these on with embroidery thread. When the figure is dry, sew on its eyes, nose and mouth.

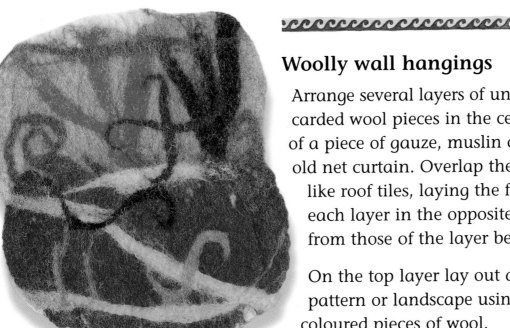

Woolly wall hangings

Arrange several layers of undyed carded wool pieces in the centre of a piece of gauze, muslin or an old net curtain. Overlap the pieces like roof tiles, laying the fibres of each layer in the opposite direction from those of the layer below.

On the top layer lay out a bold pattern or landscape using coloured pieces of wool.

Fold the material around the wool and wet it with hot soapy water. Press and rub it hard all over with your hands or a rolling pin.

When the wool has flattened, turn it over and press and rub the other side. Unwrap the material and pluck the wool fibres. If they can still be picked off, continue rubbing and pressing.

Once the felt is solid, wrap it around a stick and fasten it in place. Sprinkle on soapy water and roll and press both sides on a hard surface. Rinse it several times in warm water and leave it to dry. Sew decorative lines of stitching on the felt to strengthen it.

Tie-dyeing

More than two thousand years ago, people discovered that they could make circles or squares on cloth by bunching it up, tying thread around it and dipping it in dye.

Monica Stoppleman

In West Africa, tie-dyed patterns are bold and dramatic, as this cloth from the Ivory Coast shows. It was made from cheap white cotton, which has been dyed with indigo and kola nut juice.

The threads are tied very tightly, so that the dye cannot sink into the cloth at those points. Cloth like this is made into long flowing robes, which display the whole design. These robes are worn by both men and women.

In India, both silk and fine cotton are tied tightly with knotted threads. They are then dyed to make patterns of tiny dots and circles in vivid colours.

This girl from the dry, dusty land of Kutch, in west India, is dressed in her wedding outfit. Her lovely silk veil has been knotted and dyed by hand. Hand-knotted cloth costs far more than factory-printed imitations which people use for everyday wear.

Ketuben Rabari/ Eleinud Edwards

The women who knot the cloth grow a long pointed nail on the little finger of their left hand. They use this to poke up tiny bumps of fabric.

Collection John Gillow

Each bump is tied six or eight times with a thread which runs unbroken from bump to bump.

The ties are left on when the cloth is sold to prove it is genuinely hand-made. When the cloth is used and stretched out, the threads break.

In Japan, people carefully fold and stitch cloth to create very precise effects. This woman is wearing a gown called a *kimono*. The tie-dyed patterns on it were inspired by flower blossoms, woven mats and waves.

Women who make this cloth for a living wear a pad to protect their hands from the tough, repeated stitching.

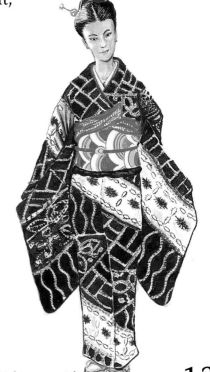

Dramatic dyeing

There are all kinds of ways to tie-dye. Choose the result you want – either random patterns of colour or something more neat, elegant and ordered.

Fancy folding

Fold a square of cloth into a quarter, roll it up and bind several rubber bands, around it as shown below.

Soak the roll thoroughly in clean water. Put it in a dye bath. The outside will be dyed the deepest colour, whilst the centre, which is most protected by layers of fabric, will be palest. Leave the roll tied to dry or rinse it in clean water, undo it and then dry it.

Surprise, surprise!

Roll a fabric square around a length of string, bunch it tightly as shown and tie the ends of the string together.

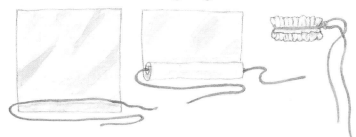

Make sure the dye bath is big enough for the whole cloth, because if you bend it, this will create a fold. When you take the cloth out of the dye, leave it bunched up to dry. Untie and iron it to fix the dye.

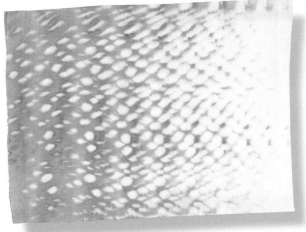

To get a dappled effect, scrunch up some cloth and tie it up before you dye it.

Triangular folds

Fold a square of fabric diagonally in half to make a triangle. Fold it in half again and then in half once more. Attach pegs to two sides and paper clips to the third side. Soak it in the dye bath.

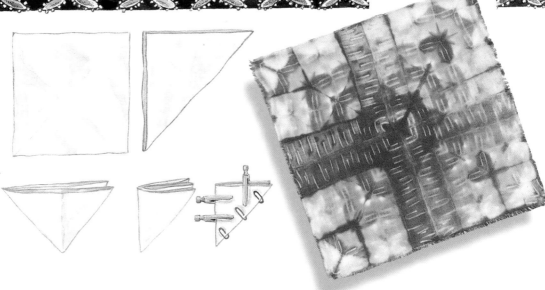

Concertina folds

Fold a square of cloth from side to side in concertina folds. Then fold the strip from top to bottom in more concertina folds to make a square.

The colour will be strongest in the outer layers. The longer you leave the fabric in the dye bath, the more even the effect will be.

Attach bulldog clips to all four corners or sides. Soak the fabric in dye.

Double dyeing

Try tie-dyeing some cloth twice. After the first dyeing, undo the folds. Let the cloth dry. Iron it and then refold, tie and dye it in a second colour. This works very well if there are large pale areas from the first dyeing.

Painted pictures

This is part of a large patterned *adire* cloth. The Yoruba people in south-west Nigeria wear these cloths wrapped around them. Every cloth shows a Yoruba saying in pictures. The symbols on this one mean 'my head is all together'.

cassava roots

indigo plant

wheel

duck

wood-louse

cocoa pods

Collection John Gillow

key

pigeon

stout bird

ostrich

The cloths are divided into squares or rectangles. The symbols painted inside the squares are part of the Yoruba picture language. They are put together in different ways to give a message.

Each artist puts a symbol, such as this bird, on the back of her cloths. This is the artist's signature.

16

1 The blue dye used to colour the cloth is made from indigo leaves which have been pounded.

2 The indigo is mixed with wood ash and water. After a few days, a blue scum forms on the surface. The liquid dye underneath is clear yellow.

3 An artist paints a design with cassava paste on undyed cotton cloth. The paste acts as a resist to stop dye colouring the design.

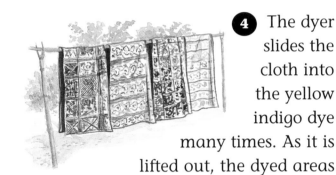

4 The dyer slides the cloth into the yellow indigo dye many times. As it is lifted out, the dyed areas turn blue. The paste is washed off.

Nicholas Barnard

This artist from Kalahasti, in south-east India, is drawing characters from the Mahabharata, an epic Hindu story. He draws with a bamboo kalam pen, which produces a line of black gum. As he presses the felt pad at the top of the pen, black gum runs down to the point.

The gum line acts as a resist. It stops the colours mixing when he paints them on later. The finished cloths decorate the walls of Hindu temples.

In the past, in Japan, images of famous warriors and battles were painted on to long cotton banners, using rice resist paste and man-made dyes. The grandparents of a newborn Samurai boy had banners made to celebrate his birth. This picture is a detail from a banner which shows Yoiche, a legendary archer, winning a battle.

Fabric painting

It's easy to paint your own fabric pictures. You will be amazed by the effects you can produce even on your first attempt. The trick is to let the fabric do the work for you.

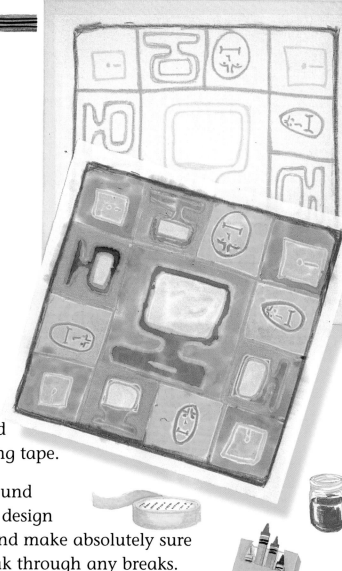

Personal pictures

Draw a simple design on paper. Repeat it several times to create a pattern. Plan the colours for your design. Stretch white cotton cloth tightly over an old wooden picture frame. Attach it with masking tape.

Using a wax crayon, draw a border around the cloth, close to the frame. Copy your design on to the centre of the cloth. Press hard and make absolutely sure there are no breaks in the lines. Dye will leak through any breaks. Ask an adult to iron it, so that the wax melts into the fabric. Protect the ironing board and iron with sheets of brown paper. Turn the frame over so the cloth does not touch the work surface.

Dip just the tip of a brush into fabric dye and touch the cloth with it, very gently. Do not paint. Watch how the cloth soaks up the dye. Use a separate brush for each colour. Repeat if necessary, but don't colour up to the wax lines. Iron the cloth again once it is dry, to fix the dyes.

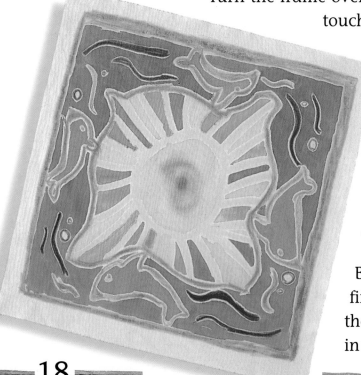

By wetting the centre of the cloth first, the artist was able to blend the yellow and orange in this picture of a sun.

Mythical figures

To paint on silk, use a fluid gum called gutta. (See stockists on page 32.)

Fasten a piece of silk as tightly as possible on to a frame. Place your frame on the table with the silk uppermost Draw a gutta border on the silk and a fantastical figure from your favourite story in the centre.

Keep squeezing and moving the gutta bottle along to create continuous lines. Remember, dye will leak through any breaks.

When your drawing is finished, leave the gutta to dry before you apply silk dye. Colour the whole picture and leave it flat to dry. Ask an adult to iron it, to fix the dyes.

Take the silk off the frame. To remove the gutta, wash the cloth gently in lukewarm soapy water. Rinse and dry it. You could use your picture as a wall-hanging or for the front of a cushion cover.

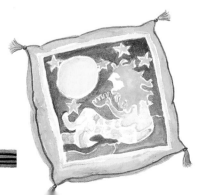

19

Block printing

The pattern on this Indian bedspread looks very complicated, but in fact there are only three different motifs. These have been printed over and over again by skilled craftsmen using carved wood blocks. Both sides of the cloth are printed with dyes which will not wash out.

Hindu motifs

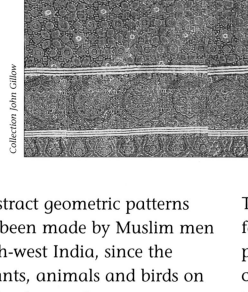

Collection John Gillow

Hindu motifs

Cloth with abstract geometric patterns like these has been made by Muslim men in Kutch, north-west India, since the 1500s. The plants, animals and birds on the wood blocks shown above are traditional motifs used by Hindus.

To create patterned cloth, white cotton fabric is put through 14 separate processes. These include bleaching in cow dung, softening with oil, dipping in tree sap, printing with blocks and dyeing with indigo, red and black dyes.

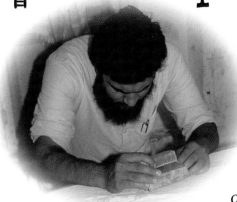

This master craftsman is printing a resist paste on to cloth to make a bedspread. He places each wood block down accurately in position to fit his design.

The paste is left to dry before the cloth is dyed. The parts of the cloth covered by the paste do not absorb any dye. The pattern is built up in several stages, using different blocks and colours.

Jabbal Khatri/ Eleinud Edwards

In Ghana, West Africa, there is a long tradition of making printed cloth with symbols like the ones below. This cloth is called *adinkra*, which means 'farewell'. In the past, adinkra cloths were worn only at funerals. Today, people wear them on important ceremonial occasions as well.

Each colour has a particular meaning. White represents purity and joy. Black is for death or extreme old age. Green is for newness and vitality. Grey is for shame and blue is for tenderness and love. Red is for serious acts of violence. Gold stands for the presence of God and the rule of the king.

Changing oneself
Playing many roles

Except God, I fear none
Symbol of the all-powerfulness and immortality of God

Moon and star
Represents royal blood and also means patience and faithfulness

Adinkra king
Chief of all the adinkra designs. Means authority grandeur and firmness

The printing blocks are carved out of pieces of calabash gourd. Each symbol stands for a well-known phrase or saying. The symbols are always printed in black.

Collection John Gillow

Printing patterns

Transform plain white cloth by printing stunning patterns on it. Look for small objects with interesting surfaces to use as printing blocks, or make your own.

Soak some string in glue and pin it in a pattern on a cork tile. Let it dry and then remove the pins. You could also stick matches on to cork, plastic or wood to make a printing block.

Mark the back of your blocks with an arrow, to show which way up to print them. Fix a piece of masking tape on the back of each block to use as a handle.

Repeating patterns

Mix acrylic paint with a little textile binder (see page 7). Paint the mixture on to a block. Press the painted block firmly on to some fabric - don't let it slide about. Take it off by turning it on to one side and raising it at the same time.

Try printing the same block again and again across the cloth or using two blocks with different colours.

Make a pattern with a variety of blocks and colours.

To make a patterned border, print different blocks in a repeated order, starting at one end.

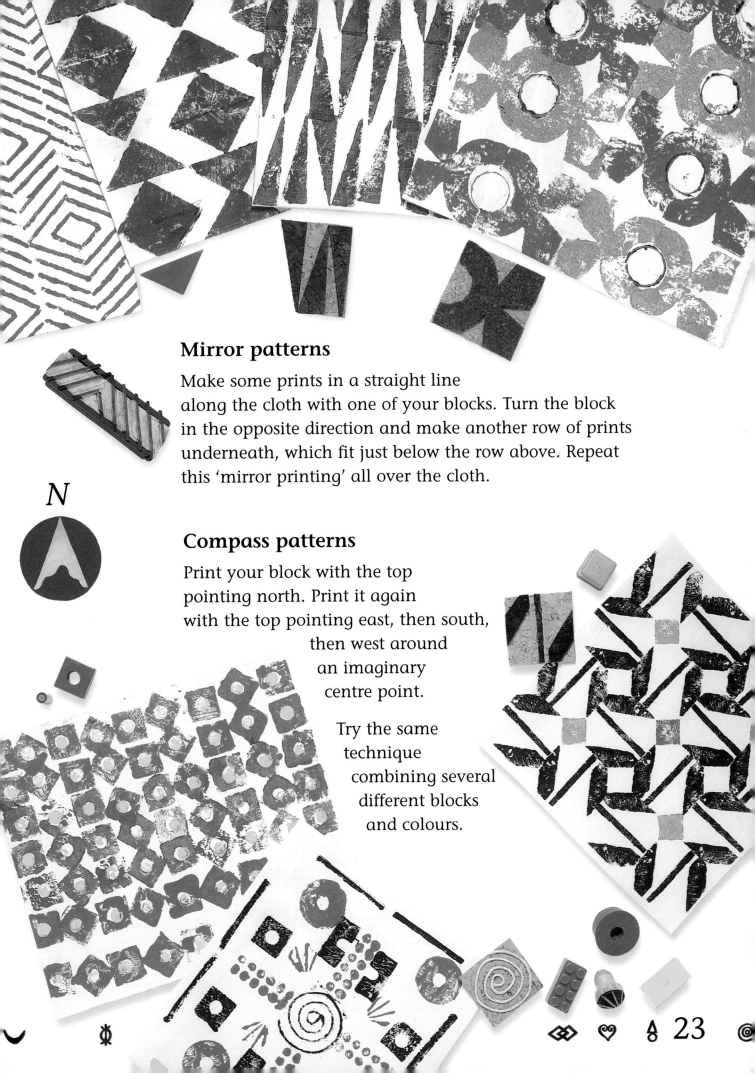

Mirror patterns

Make some prints in a straight line along the cloth with one of your blocks. Turn the block in the opposite direction and make another row of prints underneath, which fit just below the row above. Repeat this 'mirror printing' all over the cloth.

N

Compass patterns

Print your block with the top pointing north. Print it again with the top pointing east, then south, then west around an imaginary centre point.

Try the same technique combining several different blocks and colours.

New cloths from old

In Peru, Chile and Colombia, women make
brightly coloured wall-hangings and
bedspreads by sewing fabric scraps
on to a large piece of backing fabric.
This sewing technique is called *appliqué*.

This appliqué cloth is called an *arpillera*.
It was made by women in Peru and
shows a scene from their everyday life.
Hills and fields have been made from
overlapping pieces of fabric. Animals
and plants have been stitched on top.

The llama, cactus and fruits have
been padded to make them stand out.
The people were made separately and
stitched on to the picture. Sometimes
dried flowers, pieces of straw and beads
are also included.

24

In the 1970s, the army in Chile took over the government. Men who opposed the army were taken away, never to return.

Reproduced by permission of CAFOD

Women made arpilleras with scraps from the men's clothes to keep their memories alive.

Each arpillera had a message. The maker hoped people abroad would understand the message and send help – which they did.

This one shows women going to a homeless shelter. All the men are missing.

These figures are taken from a large appliqué made in north India. Each figure was cut out separately and sewn on to a plain background. The design was copied from wall-hangings which decorate the shrine of a Muslim warrior, Salar Masud. They tell the story of his victory in a famous battle.

Appliqué quilts have been made in North America since the 1600s, when America was a colony of England. The English passed a law forbidding colonists to make cloth. Colonists either had to buy cloth at great expense from England or re-use whatever they had brought with them several times over.

Women went to popular weekly meetings, called 'quilting bees' to make appliqué squares. These were joined together to make 'friendship quilts', which the women gave to each other on special occasions, such as marriage.

Cut-out pictures

Make a crazy cloth picture using fabric scraps, ribbons and shiny threads. Sketch it on paper first. When you make it in cloth, it will be in three layers – the background (the floor and walls or hills and sky), the main elements (buildings and figures) and the fine details (a smile, claws or hair).

Appliqué animals

Cut out a square or rectangle of fabric for the background. Draw an animal on thin card and cut the shape out. This is your template. Draw round the template on to a suitable fabric for your animal.

Cut out the fabric and glue it on to the background. Glue on some contrasting pieces of fabric for a tail, ears or markings. Stitch on the eyes, a nose and mouth or draw them on with a felt-tip pen.

Dazzling disco

Capture the energy of a wild disco by using a dark fabric for the background, shiny fabric for the lights and net and ribbons for the light beams. Cut out dancers from plain fabric. Glue them on to the background. Give them sparkly clothes and shoes. Draw their faces with felt-tip pens.

Cloth people

Pipe-cleaner people are simple to make. Twist two pipe-cleaners together to make a simple figure. Make the head, hands and feet out of stretchy cloth and stitch them in place. Stitch on eyes and a mouth. Cut out two pieces of fabric each for the top and the trousers and sew them around the figure. Sew on some woolly hair.

To make soft figures, stuff pieces of nylon stocking with cotton wool and stitch them together. Wind thread around the neck, waist and wrists to create the head, body and hands. Wrap felt clothes over the nylon body and stitch them in place. Draw or stitch features on the faces.

Real life drama

Think of an exciting real or imaginary story. Draw the most dramatic events as a picture.

Cut out a fabric rectangle for the background. If you want to stitch your picture, use a loose weave fabric, so that a needle will go through it easily. Cut the main shapes out of felt. Sew or glue them in place. Make separate cloth people to sew on top.

The picture above tells the story of a girl who fell out of her loft head-first. Her friend called an ambulance, which rushed her to hospital where she soon got better.

Radiant recycling

This modern wall-hanging was made by children and their parents with the help of a local artist. They used two rug-making techniques, called *hooky* and *proggy*. These techniques had almost been forgotten, but have now been revived.

Ali Rhind

Proggy rugs are made with short strips of cloth cut from old clothes. The strips are prodded through loose weave sacking. The maker works from the back of the rug, using a pointed prodder. The finished rugs are thick and shaggy.

Hooky rugs are made face up. Long strips of cloth are pulled through the sacking from the back to the front with a hook to create a flat, looped rug. Hooky rugs have more precise and detailed designs than proggy rugs.

150 years ago, hard-wearing rag rugs were made by poor communities in England, Scandinavia and on the east coast of Canada and North America. Once people could afford woven carpets, they threw their rag rugs away. Few have survived.

BEAMISH, The North of England Open Air Museum, County Durham

Making rugs used to be a communal actitivy. The men made heavy wooden frames, over which they stretched cloth sacks. The women drew designs on the sacking. On long, dreary winter days, they would sit together making rugs, while their children kept warm by the fire cutting rag strips.

Reproduced by permission of the American Museum in Britain, Bath ©

A farmer in North America made this hooked rug of a trotting horse in about 1850. She drew the horse freehand with a charred stick on a grain sack before hooking the rug with drab, worn-out clothes.

Perfect proggy rug

Make a thick, shaggy rug
to put beside your bed.

The frame and the progger

Ask an adult to help you tack 10 ounce
sacking to a wooden picture frame. Or,
buy a rug frame and follow the supplier's
instructions for attaching the hessian (see
stockists on page 32). Tighten the frame to
make the hessian taut.

Buy a progger or shape a
wooden clothes peg, like this.

A bold design

Draw and colour in a design on a piece
of paper. Use bold shapes which fill
almost all the space, with no details
smaller than a bottle top. Mark a border
4 cm from the edge of the sacking with
a felt-tip pen. Copy your design on
to the sacking in chalk. Go over it
with a thick, black felt-tip pen.

Finding fabrics

Choose heavyweight patterned or plain
cast-off fabrics with texture, such as
woollen blankets, skirts and shrunken
machine-made woollen jumpers. Select
garments of the same thickness. Cut them
into 10 cm widths across the body. Cut
these widths into 2 cm bands as shown.

Push and prod

1

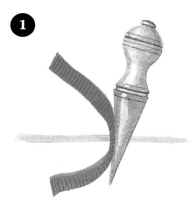

Rest part of the frame on a table with your design facing upwards. Holding your progger like a pencil, make a hole in the sacking and push one end of a cloth strip into the hole. Catch the end underneath the sacking with your free hand and pull it half-way through.

2

Make a second hole about 1 cm away. Poke the other end of the strip through this hole, so that you get a flat loop on the surface facing you. Both the ends will poke out underneath the sacking. Check that they are roughly equal lengths. The underside of the sacking will be the top side of the rug.

3

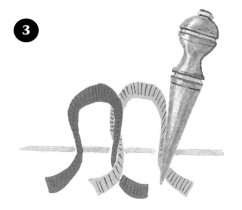

Push one end of the next strip into the same hole. Repeat the process as before until you have covered the central space. Cut through the sacking close to the frame.

4

Fold back the hessian border to create a hem. Stitch it securely to stop the edges from fraying.

Turn it over and enjoy a big surprise! Trim the surface to make the pile even all over.

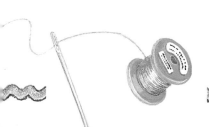

Index

Acknowledgements

The authors and publishers would like to thank the following children for their help in testing and creating the projects in this book:
Kit Evans, Avril Fech-Stewart, Ryan Macleod, Sebastian Hendry, Iona Smith and all at Sychpwll for the felt projects; Ursie Allen, Sian Anthony, Georgy Ashcroft Spurr, Luke Baldwin, Sarah Barwell, Niki Baxter, Angus Beaumont, Grace Beaumont, Josh Blackwell, Liam Blackwell, Lizzie Blount, Elizabeth Breckles, David Bullivant, Ed Casswell, Alice Chan, Patch Coole, Jacob Coupe, Daisy Crook, Natalie Crookes, Ben Davies, Oliver Davies, John Dixon, Briony Gallimore, Laura Garbett, James Gibbs, Kayleigh Graham, Matthew Graham, Christopher Greenwell, Ben Gregory, Hayden Haslam, Brendan Jackson, Emma Johnson, Joe Labellarte, Murray Lockrie, Hinnah Mahmood, Maaria Mahmood, Daniel Mason, Laurie Matarasso, Briony Mcgeorge, Joe Naylor, Rosie Needham-Smith, Richard Newbold, Bethan Pearce, Judith Posner, Miriam Posner, Hassan Price, Ian Price, David Pritchard, Stephanie Purser, Thomas Sleep, Jack Smith, Imogen Sotos-Costello, Zoe Thomas, Jessica Thorpe, Lee Wade, Laura Wardel, Jenny Williams, Callum Young, Sammy Young and staff, in particular Ann Grierson, at Lady Bay Primary School, West Bridgford, Nottingham for the painted patterns, tie-dyeing and block printing projects; Camilli Bhogal-Todd, Izzy Butcher, Faye Gale-Robinson, Rosamund Hanson, Eva Garland, Milena Kelsang for the cut-out picture projects and Toni Suggins, Mark Cuthbertson, Lee Cox, Stuart Nairn, Sarah Coughlin, Helen Bulmer, Andrew McQuiggan, Gavin Rothery, Craig, parents and staff, in particular, Andrew Westerman, at Bournmoor Primary School Co. Durham for the rug projects.

They would also like to thank the following people for providing valuable information and loaning source material: Roy Russell and Mary Eve; John Picton; Mary Burkett 'the mother of felt'; Jeff Higley; Eleinud Edwards; Jeremy Farrell of the Nottingham Costume Museum; John Gillow; Mo Fini, Ali Shapter and Lucy Davies of TUMI; Jennifer Matthews; John and Helen Blackmore.

Stockists

Dyes:
• M & R Dyes, Carters, Station Road, Wickham Bishops, Witham, Essex. CM8 3JB. Tel: 01621 891405/0860 906335 Fax: 01621 893528
• Dylon International Ltd, London, SE26 5HD Tel: 0181 663 4801
Widely stocked by haberdashers and art shops

Acrylics, textile binders, silk dyes, gutta and applicators
• Available from specialist craft shops.
• Mail order from Specialist Crafts Ltd., P.O. Box 247, Leicester LE1 9QS

Pad and block printing materials
• Dryad P.O. Box 38, Northgates, Leicester LE1 9BU

Ready-carded wool
• Wool Work Freepost, 70 Main St, Wentworth, Rotherham, S.Yorks Tel 01226 742926 Fax 01226 741166
• The Cotswold Woollen Weavers, Filkins, near Lechdale, Glos.

Proggy rug supplies (including booklets, frames, tools and equipment)
• Ali Rhind Design Studio, Ouseburn Warehouse, 36 Lime Street, Newcastle upon Tyne NE1 2PN Tel and fax: 0191 2332121

Rug tools
• Fred Aldous, 37 Lever Street, Manchester M60 1UX Tel: 0161 236 2477

South American artefacts and information
• Tumi, 8/9, New Bond Street Place, Bath, Avon. BA1 1BH Tel: 01225 462367; Fax: 01225 444870